LITTLE CHIEF® brand

home **electric smoker**

- ## RECIPES
- ## OPERATING INSTRUCTIONS*

Published for your enjoyment by
LUHR·JENSEN and SONS, INC.

*See Page 40

Dedicated to the Gourmet Cook, the
Adventuresome Sportsman and the
hearty and appreciative appetites
of all their friends.

LITTLE CHIEF ®
brand

contents

1

2

contents
(continued)

foreword

The recipes and information in this book were developed while using the "Little Chief" electric smoker and the four varieties of "Chips 'n Chunks" wood flavor fuels.

In the 15 years that we have manufactured the "Little Chief," we've smoked just about every type of food imaginable. (And some that were not.) We have sampled many types of flavor fuels to determine which would serve us best. Type of wood, its quality, and the texture of the processed wood are all important to the finished product. Temperature and air-flow characteristics of the "Little Chief" have been tested and charted under different operating conditions and the unit's design has been modified and improved several times over the years. We've had assistance and design suggestions from a good many people. Gourmet cooks and smoking enthusiasts, just like yourself, from all over the world have contributed to the quality and reliability of the "Little Chief."

The "Little Chief" has been a fun-filled adventure for us at Luhr Jensen. Smoke delicacies seem to be an everyday experience as our company "family" and friends are constantly trying for a new or more exotic taste treat. Over the years we have accumulated numerous recipes from our own experiments with the smoker and from our many customers and friends who want to share their own successful secrets. In a word, the "Little Chief" smoker has been FUN!...As it will be for you as the mysteries of unique food preparation techniques unfold and become a part of your culinary style.

After a brief explanation of the basics of "curing" and the fundamentals of what the smoke generating "Little Chief" can do, we will move on to a selection of recipes that are guaranteed to excite your palate and imagination.

4

anatomy of smoke cooking and curing!

Back to Basics

When you really think about it, just how far back does the "curing" of meats go? If you didn't have a refrigerator or a freezer, what would *you* do to preserve the necessary foodstuffs for your family? One doesn't have to exercise this point very long to determine that the early day inhabitants of this grand planet earth must have given a lot of serious consideration to this question.

No doubt the earliest Neolithic methods were a simple drying process done by the sun and the wind. As fire was used to aid the drying and cooking, it was discovered that the foods prepared in this manner tasted better and had greater lasting qualities.

At a later time, the process of "salting" the meat, prior to smoking, was discovered. The historical significance of this discovery cannot be overemphasized.

Salting or the infusion of salt into meat of various types is called "curing." Simply stated, this process causes the meat to undergo certain physical, chemical and bacteriological changes which result in greatly extended stability. More specifically, salt (sodium chloride) acts to suppress the growth of spoilage causing bacteria and to solubize the available meat proteins. With the introduction of salt to a cut of meat, the meat proteins dissolve and the meat becomes tacky. When heated, the dissolved proteins set up and "bind" the meat. This phenomena is most important in the manufacture of sausage or heavily-cured meats such as pork or certain dried fish products.

Other chemical elements are sometimes introduced into commercially cured foodstuffs to control color and texture. We need not, quite happily in fact, bother ourselves with these extra and somewhat controversial chemicals.

**3 Ways
...or the
"Real Cure"**

The science (and art) of "curing" is simply the infusion of salt into your food products, which can be achieved by three different methods:

(1) THE COVER BRINE...which is the easiest of the three and the most applicable to what we are trying to accomplish. Most recipes and suggested cycle times in this booklet use the cover brine system.

(2) THE DRY CURE...excellent for old-fashioned curing of hams and bacon. This process is still used by some specialty sales firms in the southeast. It is, however, a time-consuming and rather costly process, unless done on a large volume or on a commercial basis.

(3) INJECTION CURE...used almost exclusively by commercial meat packers. It is fast and effective, allowing the processing firms to speed processing and lower in-house inventories. It is, however, complicated and much too sophisticated for the home processer.

The cover brine can do it all for us. Making the assumption that our quantities of food are going to be processed in the "Little Chief" smoker, these same quantities can easily be "brined" in a glass, crockery or plastic container that will allow the brine solution to completely cover the food.

Other benefits of this process become immediately apparent. It is easy to vary the salt concentration of the brine solution and it is easy to introduce other taste variations such as spices, herbs, or a variety of fruit juices. The blending of these various tastes (along with the inherent taste of the meat product you are processing) is what it's all about. At this point I think it is fair to say that the possibilities of achieving a wide variety of subtle, yet distinctive taste varieties becomes readily apparent.

6

**Heat
and Smoke
Processing
Your Product**

The previous section outlined the traditional "curing" systems. The next step in our total process is the application of warm, dry air to the product. What happens to the cured meats during heat processing?

(1) The meat loses some of its moisture.
(2) It becomes pasteurized if the temperature is raised above 145.°
(3) The proteins coagulate and set up to "bind" the product.
(4) The cured meat color develops.

Without getting into rather complicated explanations regarding temperature, heat transfer, humidity, and surface evaporation, suffice it to say that your "Little Chief" smoker has been "factory tuned" to provide exactly the proper temperature and air flow to:

(1) Remove moisture quickly.
(2) Raise internal temperature of your product to approximately 165.°
(3) AND FINALLY, to provide an efficient and reliable smoke generator that will supply the "OLD-FASHIONED" smoke flavors to the various foodstuffs that you are processing.

This smoke vapor not only marvelously flavors these foodstuffs, but provides certain chemicals that penetrate the surface and assist in controlling the growth of the various micro-organisms which are the principal causes of decay.

Warning!

Although the described methods of curing and smoking will flavor your foodstuffs and will inhibit or stop natural deterioration, they are not a magic process that will restore freshness and good flavor to food that is already tainted. It is a waste of time and materials to process foods that have already lost their freshness and flavor. The little extra effort taken to bring a fresh product to your smoker will pay big dividends in the quality of the finished product.

basic brines and seasonings and important suggestions

Herbs

Spices

Many of the recipes you will find in this book will refer to the "EASY-CURE" brine solution. It is a simple and effective way to brine fish, poultry, wild game, or butcher meats. It also provides a base from which to expand with other seasonings or juices.

"EASY-CURE" brine solution

½ cup NON-iodized salt
½ cup white household sugar
1 quart of good quality water

Mix ingredients in a quartjar, ½ full of warm water. When thoroughly mixed, fill the jar to the brim with cold tap water. If solution is not used immediately, store it in the refrigerator (the cooler the better).

To emphasize the simplicity of the smoke-curing process, it would be fair to say that ALL fish, meat, or poultry can be deliciously prepared using the "EASY-CURE" brine and the "LITTLE CHIEF" smoker. Only the cycle times in the brine and the smoker would vary, depending on the type of meat and your personal taste.

Easy and terrific! Now that you have mastered the simple art of basic curing, you are ready to move on to bigger and better things. The following chapters are chock full of recipes you will enjoy. Sample them—and add your own favorite flavor touches. Below are listed some of the suggested seasonings you will find useful in developing some of your own brines and marinades.

Herbs:	Spices:	Other:
Basil	Caraway	Garlic
Bay	Cayenne	Onion
Dill	Celery Seed	Monosodium Glutomate
Oregano	Cloves	Kitchen Bouquet
Marjoram	Curry	Maggi Seasoning
Parsley	Ginger	
Rosemary	Mace	
Sage	Nutmeg	
Terregon	Pepper	
Thyme	Tumeric	

Natural Sugars and Juices and Special Seasoning Sauces

Honey (various types)
Molasses
Brown Sugar
Apple Juice
Pineapple Juice
Orange Juice
Lemon Juice
Wines and Sherries
Berry Juices
Rum

Worcestershire
Tabasco
Chili Sauce
Soy
Catsup
A-1 Sauce

Important Suggestions

Brines should be mixed throughly in glass, crockery, or plastic vessels. Wooden or aluminum containers ARE NOT TO BE USED.

A large spoon and a glass quart jar are handy for mixing the "EASY-CURE" brine. Meats should be completely immersed in the brine, and they should be stirred or rearranged in the solution occasionally.

Keep brines as cool as possible. If you plan to reuse them, store them in the refrigerator. Reuse should be limited to 2 or 3 times only and a storage period of no longer than 1 week is recommended.

After brining, give your meat a light rinse in cool water and allow it to air dry for about an hour before putting it into the smoker. You will notice a glossy look to the meat or fish when it is dry. This is called the "pellicle" and its formation on the surface of your meat is important.

As stated in your "Little Chief" instructional booklet, it is a good practice to pre-heat your smoker for 15 minutes prior to use. Load the smoker rack at your preparation area and transport the rack to the outside smoking site, loading and fueling of the smoker is completely illustrated on the "Here's How" page of your instructional booklet.

curing and smoking fish and shellfish

It is important that we understand the difference between the smoking and the drying portions of the processing cycle. In many cases, the recipes call for a total drying time of 6 to 12 hours or more, while saying, also, that the recipe calls for only 2 panfuls of flavor fuel. This means that your smoker will only be "smokin" for about 2 hours, but the product needs much more total drying time in the unit to complete the full curing cycle. While your product may need, or be able to absorb, only so much of the smoke flavor, it indeed needs much more drying time to bring it to the desired state of "doneness."

Smoking Fish

There are so many wonderful fish and shellfish available it seems a shame that we can't deal with each of them in a very specific manner. Their delicate flavors lend themselves to the light touches of herbs and natural sweeteners. The recipes that follow will give you insight into the ways they can be deliciously prepared. Let's start with a list of some of the fish with which our "Easy Cure" brine solution will work.

Freshwater Fish	Saltwater Fish	Shellfish
Bass	Barracuda	Clams
Bream	Bass	Crayfish
Carp	Bonefish	Mussels
Crappie	Bonita	Scallops
Catfish	Cod	Shrimp
Grayling	Corbina	Oysters
Kokanee	Dolphin	Etc.
Musky	Flounder	
Perch	Grouper	
Pike	Grunt	
Shad	Halibut	
Sturgeon	Herring	
Steelhead	Mackerel	
Trout (all types)	Mullet	
Etc.	Octopus	
	Pompano	
	Snook	
	Squid	
	Salmon (all types)	
	Tuna	
	Yellowtail	
	Wahoo	
	Etc.	

10

Important Suggestions When Preparing Fish to Smoke

Handle your fish carefully in the many processes necessary to get them to your dining table. You will have a better product if your fish is not bruised or mistreated in the catching, cleaning, and preparing stages.

Proper field dressing and cooling is imperative. Smoke-curing won't restore freshness lost because of poor handling. Clean your fish as quickly as possible, and cool them with a grass evaporation pack or bag, or on ice if it's available.

If your fish must be held for some time before smoking, they should be quickly frozen. Small fish can be totally immersed in water or a light saline solution (1 Tbsp salt to a quart of water) and brought to 0° F. by a good cold freezer. Larger fish can be cleaned and sectioned into convenient chunks that will fit into a ½ gallon milk container and quickly frozen in the saline solution.

You will notice that the partially frozen fish is much easier to handle and to cut. Try a stiff sharp knife on your semi-frozen fish. It's like cutting balsa wood.

Depending on the size and thickness of your fish, you may elect to:

(1) Prepare for processing by cutting fish into chunks, completely deboning as you go.
(2) Filet your fish with a thin knife, cutting above the bone layer to eliminate further deboning and then smoke the whole or portioned filet.
(3) Simply remove the entrails and head, and smoke the remaining fish whole. (Smaller fish such as smelt, herring, small trout or kokanee.) If you hang the whole fish in your smoker, be sure to prop open the belly cavity with a toothpick.

Lastly, be sure your prepared chunk filets or whole fish have been neatly prepared so that they are nicely presentable when done. Cut away all unsightly material and wash the product thoroughly before brining or placing in the smoker.

The "STEP BY STEP INSTRUCTIONS" (page 41 of this instruction booklet) pictorially illustrates the exact way to prepare a salmon (or any larger fish), using the "Easy-Cure" brine method and the "Little Chief" electric smoker.

You may nicely store your smoked fish in aluminum foil or a tightly covered plastic container in the refrigerator, for up to 4 weeks. (If it lasts that long.) The longer the drying process, the longer it will keep.

"Easy Cure" Smoked Fish

1.

1 qt. water
½ cup non-iodized salt
½ cup white sugar

Fill a quart jar ½ full with good warm water. Add salt and sugar. Mix well until dissolved. Top off jar with cold water. This recipe may be increased if you need more brine.

Immerse prepared fish chunks, filets or small whole fish completely in the brine solution.

Brine chunks 1" thick, 8 to 12 hours or overnight. Brine filets to ½" thick about 4 hours and small whole fish or very thin pieces about 2 to 4 hours.

Stir solution and rotate fish occasionally. Remove from brine. Rinse each piece in cool water and place on paper towels. Pat dry.

In about 1 hour, you will notice a tacky glaze on the surface of the fish. This is called the "pellicle." Your fish is now ready for loading into the smoker.

THICK CHUNKS—Smoke 8 to 12 hours, using 3 panfuls of Chips 'n Chunks flavor fuel.
FILETS TO ½"—Smoke 5 to 8 hours, using 2 panfuls of Chips 'n Chunks flavor fuel.
SMALL FISH, THIN PIECES—Smoke 2 to 4 hours, using 1 or 2 panfuls of Chips 'n Chunks flavor fuel.

Add Chips 'n Chunks during early stages of the drying cycle. Check the meat periodically for the degree of doneness you desire.

"Little Chief" Smoked Fish #2

(for oily fish with a stronger flavor)

2.

2 qts. water
1 cup non-iodized salt
½ cup brown sugar
2 Tbsp lemon concentrate
or ¼ cup lemon juice
¼ Tbsp garlic powder
¼ Tbsp onion powder

Use small fish or filet of large.

Mix all ingredients and stir until dissolved.

Brine fish 4 or more hours. Rinse and dry. Rack and load.

Use 3 to 5 panfuls Hickory, Apple or Alder. Keep in the smoker 4 to 10 hours, depending on the size of fish pieces.

(Use this recipe for: Cod, Bass, Pike, Tuna types, Sturgeon, Barracuda, Mackerel, Eels, and for Squid and Octopus.)

"Little Chief" Smoked Salmon Deluxe

(Chinook, Coho, etc.)

3.

Brine:
- ⅓ cup sugar
- ¼ cup non-iodized salt
- 2 cups soy sauce
- 1 cup water
- ½ tsp onion powder
- ½ tsp garlic powder
- ½ tsp pepper
- ½ tsp tabasco sauce
- 1 cup dry white wine

Brine salmon chunks 8 or more hours, keeping refrigerated.

Fill flavor pan with Hickory, Alder, or mix ⅔ Apple with ⅓ Cherry. Use 2 to 3 panfuls. Leave in the smoker until drying is completed. This may take 12 hours, depending on the thickness of the meat. Place largest and thickest chunks on the bottom rack.

(Also use for Steelhead and other large trout.)

"Little Chief" Smokey Smelt

(the beer-drinker's friend)

4.

Brine:
- 1 cup non-iodized salt
- 1 cup brown sugar
- 1 cup soy sauce
- ½ cup cider vinegar
- 1 Tbsp Worcestershire sauce
- 1 Tbsp paprika
- 1 Tbsp chili powder
- 1 Tbsp garlic salt (optional)
- 1 Tbsp onion salt
- ½ tsp pepper
- 3 cups warm water

Some prefer whole smelt, others remove heads and entrails with a pair of scissors. Either way, wash smelt in clear water.

Mix all ingredients in warm water. Let the brine cool and add the smelt. Brine the smelt 4 or more hours. Rinse and air dry.

Use 3 panfuls of Apple, Alder or Hickory flavor fuel. Keep in the smoker until done. (5 to 7 hours.)

"Little Chief" Smoked Clams

Open your clams by steaming in a kettle. Shake the clam meat from its shell. Split the neck and cut out the stomach with scissors. Wash the clam in cold water, picking out any noticeable sand particles from the meat.

5. Place clams in the "EASY CURE" brine solution for 30 minutes. Rinse lightly in warm water and allow to air dry for 40 minutes.

Place on an oiled screen in your "LITTLE CHIEF" and smoke for 2 hours using 2 pans of Alder or Apple Chips 'n Chunks flavor fuel.

"Little Chief" Smoked Oysters

After removal from its shell, the oyster should be blanched. Cut larger oysters into smaller pieces. Blanching is easy. Simply put the oysters in a metal strainer and dip them into boiling water until the edges curl. (Usually 2 to 3 minutes.) Then rinse in cool tap water.

6. Place oysters in the "EASY CURE" brine solution for 40 minutes. Rinse lightly in warm water and allow to air dry for 40 minutes.

Place oysters on an oiled screen in your "LITTLE CHIEF" and smoke for 50 to 75 minutes. They are done when the edges look dry. Try one. If they get overcooked they become a bit chewy. Use Alder or Apple Chips 'n Chunks flavor fuel.

"Little Chief" Smoked Shrimp, Prawns and Crayfish

If your shrimp is uncooked, peel and pre-cook them in bouillon for 5 minutes. Place the meat in the "EASY CURE" brine solution for 2 hours. Rinse under tap water and arrange on paper towels for drying. Allow to air dry for 40 minutes.

7. Place meat on an oiled screen in your "LITTLE CHIEF" and smoke for 2 hours, using 2 pans of Alder or Apple Chips 'n Chunks flavor fuel.

Jiffy Smoked Fish Patties

8.

2 cups flaked fish (canned or left overs)
2 beaten eggs
1 cup bread crumbs or crackers (smoked if you like)
1 Tbsp minced onion
dash pepper
salt to taste

Place fish in a greased baking dish that will fit into your "LITTLE CHIEF," spreading evenly and loosely in the dish.

Smoke for 1 panful of Hickory or Alder Chips 'n Chunks flavor fuel and allow to cool.

Mix ingredients thoroughly. Mold into patties and fry in hot butter or bacon grease until golden brown. These are great on toast with white sauce, or make a smoked fishburger with all the trimmings. Yum!

Smoked Salmon or Tuna Spread

9.

For sandwiches that are a real treat, drain the liquid from canned salmon or canned tuna. Place in a greased baking dish that will fit easily into the Little Chief smoker. Flake fish with a fork, spreading it out over the dish. Place in your preheated smoker and smoke for one hour or the time it takes for one pan of Apple or Alder flavor fuel to exhaust itself. Remove from smoker. Allow to cool.

Prepare your favorite sandwich spread with smoked flavored fish.

Smoked Salmon and Cream Cheese Omelet

10.

Saute 2 chopped green onions and ⅓ cup smoked salmon in butter for 2 or 3 minutes. Stir in cubed cream cheese (3 oz. package) until melted.

Use to fill 2 3-egg omelets.

Smokey Salmon Nuggets

11.

2 cups flaked, smoked salmon
1½ cups seasoned mashed potatoes
1 egg, beaten slightly
1 tsp grated onion
dash pepper
½ cup fine cornflake crumbs
oil for deep-fat frying

Combine fish, potatoes, egg, onion, and pepper. Beat until smooth. Chill well.

Portion fish mixture with a ¼ cup measure. Shape into balls. Roll in crumbs. Fry in hot, deep fat, 350° F., 3 to 5 minutes or until thoroughly heated and lightly browned.

Serve hot with your favorite egg or cheese sauce. Makes 12 balls. Approximately 4 servings.

smoke flavoring of meats

The smoke flavoring of meats is simply a delight!…and delightfully simple! Aside from the processing of jerky, or the manufacture of corned beef, where a strong cure is desired, we simply use the "LITTLE CHIEF" smoker as a smoke-generator for application of smoke flavors. You may then prepare these various cuts in your own favorite way.

We will provide some suggestions for you to start with…some with interesting and exciting marinades that you will enjoy very much.

Please remember that smoke flavoring is NOT a curing process. Your meats must be cooked, refrigerated or frozen immediately after the smoke flavoring.

When smoke flavoring it is good to pre-heat the smoker and have a dense smoke already generated before placing the meat inside. This should take less than 15 minutes.

There are 4 different "CHIPS 'N CHUNKS" flavor fuels available to you, and, like other seasonings, your preferences are a highly personal thing. We will recommend those that we like, but don't hesitate to experiment to suit *YOUR* taste.

Steaks, Chops and Ribs

1. In your pre-heated and smoking "LITTLE CHIEF," place these cuts for 20 minutes. Use HICKORY or ALDER "CHIPS 'N CHUNKS," then prepare in your favorite way. Shorten your cooking time by 20% on these smaller cuts, as the smoking time will start your cooking process.

Roasts: Beef, Pork or Lamb

2. In your pre-heated and smoking "LITTLE CHIEF," place these thicker cuts for 20 minutes per pound and 2 hours maximum. Try cherry or hickory on beef, and apple on pork or lamb. Prepare in your favorite way. Shorten your cooking time by 10%.

Sliced Bacon, Canadian Bacon, Ham Slices, Link Sausage

3. In your pre-heated and smoking "LITTLE CHIEF," place these cuts for 20 minutes. These meats seem to beg for the more tangy flavors of hickory and alder, but also try the apple if you would like a slightly sweeter and smoother flavor.

Country Sausage

4. Prepare exactly as above, but try the cherry "CHIPS 'N CHUNKS." You are guaranteed comment! Smoke for 10 minutes the first time. You can try more later, if it turns you on.

Hamburger

5. Use for patties, meat loaf, meat balls, chili, hash or other "hamburger helpers."

Spread your ground beef in a shallow pan or on a fine screen (preferably) and place into your pre-heated and smoking "LITTLE CHIEF" for 20 minutes. Hickory and alder are zippy...apple is a bit more mellow...and cherry will hit 'em where it counts. Take your pick. Then use the smoke flavored hamburger in your regular way. Shorten your cooking time by 20%. (Use cherry flavor when making chili; it really fits.)

■ **Now Let's Try Some Special Hamburger Recipes**

Smoke Flavored Cheese Patties

6. 3 lbs ground beef
slices of cheddar or velveeta cheese
1 package of dry onion soup mix
1 tsp pepper
Salt (to taste)

Mix all ingredients well and form into *THIN* patties. Smoke patties in pre-heated and smoking "LITTLE CHIEF" for 30 minutes. Sandwich cheese slices between smoked patties and crimp the edges. Lightly grill, salting to taste. Serve to the family hamburger king for further processing.

**Smoked
Hamburgers
Royale**

7.

2 lbs ground beef
1 egg
1 large onion,
    minced finely
20 soda crackers crushed
    to crumbs
¼ cup burgundy or heavy
    red wine
1 tsp salt
1 tsp pepper

Smoke 2 lbs hamburger as in item #5 above. Then quickly blend with other ingredients. Make large, thick patties and grill to taste. Serve a la carte, with mushroom sauce, or with buns for a "ROYALE BURGER." YUM!

**Smoked
Hamburger
Loaf**

8.

2 lbs ground beef
1 can tomato soup
1 egg
½ cup minced onion
2 Tbsp chopped parsley
1 Tbsp Worcestershire
    sauce
½ cup bread or cracker
    crumbs
1 tsp salt
dash pepper

Smoke 2 lbs of ground beef as in item #5 above. Then quickly blend with other ingredients. Shape firmly into a loaf and place into a shallow pan. Bake at 325° for 1½ hours.

**"Little Chief"
Smokey
Drumsticks**

9.

1 lb. ground beef
1 egg, well beaten
½ cup smoked fine bread
    crumbs
¼ cup finely chopped
    onions
1 tsp salt
½ tsp M.S.G.
dash pepper
4 Tbsp fat or shortening

Smoke 1 lb. of ground beef as in item #5 above. Quickly mix with other ingredients. Divide into 4 portions and shape around a 6″ skewer. Roll each, pressing lightly into smoked fine bread crumbs. Heat fat in skillet. Cook drumsticks over moderate heat, turning to evenly brown all sides. Continue cooking and turning about 15 minutes or until done.

18

With your Little Chief Smoker and inexpensive hamburger (25% fat) you can make delicious salami for picnics, snacks or sandwiches. Quickly and easily prepared. With experimentation you can vary or change spices to your own taste. You can use beef, venison, elk, bear or other hamburger meats to make this delicious salami—you will enjoy the results.

Try these recipes to start:

Smokey Hamburger Salami

(three versions)

10a

5 lbs Hamburger
5 tsp (rounded) Curing Salt*
1-1/2 tsp Garlic Powder
1-1/2 tsp Onion Powder
2-1/2 Tbls Whole Black Pepper
2 Tbls Whole Mustard Seed
2 Tbls Brown Sugar (Optional)
3 Tbls Dry Red Wine

10b

5 lbs Hamburger
5 tsp (rounded) Curing Salt*
4 Tbls White Dry Wine
1-1/2 tsp Garlic Powder
2-1/2 Tbls Chili Powder
2-1/4 tsp Crushed Red Pepper
1-1/4 tsp Ground Cumin
2 Tbls Brown Sugar (Optional)

10c

5 lbs Hamburger
5 tsp (rounded) Curing Salt*
3 Tbls Dry Red Wine
1-1/4 tsp Garlic Powder
2-1/4 Tbls Mustard Seed (Whole)
1-1/2 Tbls Sweet Basil
1-1/2 Tbls Oregano
3/4 Cup grated Parmesan Cheese
2 Tbls Brown Sugar (Optional)

Mix all ingredients thoroughly then cover and chill 24 hours or more. Divide into 4 portions.

Roll portions into 2-1/3"-3" diameter rolls and wrap with inexpensive large hole nylon net. Tie ends securely with string (net may be omitted —but, rolls flatten out while smoking).

Place in Little Chief Smoker 8-12 hours and smoke with 6-8 panfuls of Chips N Chunks.

Remove from Smoker—Remove netting and dry thoroughly with paper towel.

Wrap in foil and refrigerate up to 3 weeks or freeze up to 6 months.

It is so easy to make you don't have to make large quantities and store.

*Use only tender quick or prepared curing salt. Regular salt does not have the flavors, taste or nitrates added for the quick cure and binding of meat required to make these recipes successful. You may purchase prepared curing salts sold by Mortons, Lowery's and other companies. Check your local supermarkets, butcher shops, wine stores or feed stores. You may order from: Morton Salt Co.—Send $2.25 for 2 lbs (Dept. SM Box 355, Argo, Ill. 60501).

The Use of Marinades With Your Meat Recipes Will Add More Dimension to Your Cooking Prowess. Let These Marinades and Other Recipes Tickle Your Palate.

Fiesta Marinade

(for beef, pork or lamb roasts)

10.

Use ½ recipe for beef steaks.

2 cups red wine
½ cup soy sauce
1 Tbsp Worcestershire sauce
½ tsp tabasco sauce
½ tsp onion powder
½ tsp ground black pepper
1 Tbsp non-iodized salt
4 Tbsp cooking oil
3 Tbsp lemon juice

Mix all ingredients well. Add meat and marinade in the refrigerator for 6 hours. (Up to 12 hours won't hurt, but keep it cool.) Remove from marinade, pat dry with paper towel (don't rinse) and place into smoker as in items #1 and #2 above.

Then cook in your regular fashion. Lightly apply marinade to meat while cooking, as convenient.

Sportsman's Marinade — Teriyaki

(for beef, game, or mutton)

11.

½ cup soy sauce
¼ cup white wine
2 cloves garlic, crushed
2 Tbsp sugar
small piece fresh ginger or
1 Tbsp ground ginger

Mix ingredients well. Add meat and marinate 4 hours or more. Remove from marinade and pat dry with paper towels.

Place in smoker and smoke as in recipe #1 or #2 of this chapter.

Cook, basting lightly with marinade. Broil or roast or barbecue.

20

Creole Beef Marinade

(for beef steaks and roasts)

12.

¼ cup oil
¼ cup bourbon or sherry
2 Tbsp soy sauce
1 tsp Worcestershire sauce
1 tsp garlic powder
several twists of the pepper mill

Mix all ingredients well. Add meat and marinate up to 12 hours in the refrigerator. Remove from marinade. Pat dry with paper towels and place in smoker as in recipes #1 and #2 in this chapter. Cook in your favorite way. Lightly apply marinade to meat while cooking.

"Little Chief" Smokey Barbecued Ribs

(Beef or Spare Ribs)

13.

Sauce:
¼ cup vinegar
½ cup water
2 Tbsp sugar
1 Tbsp prepared mustard
½ tsp pepper
1½ tsp salt
¼ tsp cayenne pepper
1 thick slice of lemon
1 sliced onion
¼ cup butter
½ cup catsup
2 Tbsp Lea & Perrins

Cut ribs into serving pieces and place into pre-heated and smoking Little Chief for 1 hour. Use Hickory or Alder. (Cherry if you are from Texas; we don't offer mesquite.) Remove from smoker and place in baking pan. Pour sauce over ribs and cook for 1½ hours at 350° or until done.

In a sauce pan, mix all ingredients except the catsup and Lea & Perrins. Simmer uncovered for 20 minutes. Add remaining ingredients and bring to a boil. Use for charcoaling ribs, chicken or lamb.

"Little Chief" Smokey Pork Loin

14.

1 good quality 5 lb. pork loin
rosemary
garlic
non-iodized salt
fresh ground pepper

Trim loin ready to serve and rub an equal mixture of the above into the meat as best you can. Place in pan and let it stand in the refrigerator for 1 hour.

Place it in your Little Chief Smoker and smoke 2 hours using 2 panfuls of Chips 'n Chunks Apple Flavor.

Roast in oven at 300° for 1½ hours or until done.

Wild Things for Wild Game

15.

Brine:
1 pt. cider vinegar
1 qt. water
1 cup non-iodized salt
1 Tbsp black peppercorns
½ cup brown sugar
1 blade mace
2 Tbsp butter
¼ Tbsp parsley
2 medium onions, chopped
1 medium sliced carrot
1 cup dry red wine

Bring all ingredients, except wine, to a boil. Turn to simmer for 30 minutes. Strain into a large container and add wine. Use immediately. Do not store.

Brine meat 3 or 4 days turning often and keeping refrigerated.

Place in smoker using 2 to 5 panfuls of Hickory or Cherry "Chips 'n Chunks" flavor fuel (depending on the thickness of the meat).

Finish cooking on broiler or in the oven.

Use this recipe for: venison, elk, moose, bear, horsemeat, antelope, sheep, and reindeer.

---

* Please note that any of the aforementioned marinades will work wonderfully well with wild game cuts; either roasts or steaks. *This* recipe is especially applicable if you are a bit sensitive to the flavor of the particular cut you are preparing.

Smoked Liver

16.

Brine:
4 cups water
2 tsp salt (non-iodized)
1 tsp sugar

Use beef, veal or lamb liver sliced 1″ thick or whole chicken livers.

Soak liver in mild brine for 30 minutes. Remove and pat dry with paper towels.

Place in Little Chief smoker for 30 minutes. Use Hickory or Cherry flavor. Brush with oil. Sprinkle with garlic or onion, salt and pepper. Broil on grill (oven or charcoal) for 15 minutes. Turn once. Do not overcook.

hard curing of meats

(Hams, bacon, sausages beef and jerky)

As previously discussed in the "Back to Basics" section of this book and again in the previous chapter on smoke-flavoring, the hard curing of meats as was needed before refrigeration no longer has a pertinent application. To infuse so much salt into a product and to make it so dry that one has to boil it for a period to overcome these preservation techniques, simply doesn't make sense. A simple smoke-flavoring and refrigeration is marvelously adequate for our needs.

Hard cured beef, sometimes referred to as "corned beef," heart, kidney, tongue and other meats were also prepared in a similar fashion. The preparation of these beef and pork products require special equipment and techniques and are best handled by a professional or a highly experienced novice.

One happy exception to these facts is JERKY. We can safely and with confidence make delicious jerky from many different meats and in several different ways.

■ **Let's Try Some of These Delicious Recipes!**

"Easy Cure" Meat Jerky

1.

5 lb. meat (any cut, including wild game)
½ cup non-iodized salt
½ cup sugar
1 qt. water

Trim all fat from the meat. Slice meat *with* the grain as thin as possible. The meat slices nicely when semi-frozen, or your butcher will do the slicing for you. Place the meat in cool brine and refrigerate overnight.

After no less than 12 hours, take the meat from the brine, rinse lightly and allow to dry on paper towels for 1 hour.

Place meat strips on the smoker racks and dry for 12 hours, using 2 panfuls of Alder Chips 'n Chunks in the early stages of the drying cycle.

AT THIS POINT I would like to point out how easy it is to modify this basic jerky recipe to best suit your personal taste. If you prefer it saltier, simply don't rinse off the brine solution. If you would like to add spices or herbs, lightly sprinkle pepper, garlic, onion powder, etc. on the meat before placing it into the smoker. If you would prefer it drier, leave it in the smoker for a longer drying cycle. Of course you can use other flavor fuels such as Hickory, Apple, or Cherry. You are the Master Chef.

Well dried jerky can be stored for a long time. A glass jar with holes in the lid is a perfect container. The cool dry air in your refrigerator is the perfect environment.

But, small quantities don't last long anyway!

"Little Chief" Beef and Game Jerky

2.

Marinade/Brine in
⅓ cup sugar
¼ cup salt
2 cups soy sauce
1 cup water
1 cup red wine
½ tsp onion powder
½ tsp pepper
½ tsp garlic powder
½ tsp tabasco sauce

Trim all fat from meat. Slice meat with the grain about ¼″ to ½″ thick. The meat slices nicely when semi-frozen, or your butcher will slice it for you in his machine. Place meat in the cool marinade and leave overnight, or for no less than 8 hours.

Remove from brine and allow to air dry without rinsing. Smoke in your "LITTLE CHIEF" for 12 to 16 hours, depending on how dry you like your product. Use 3 panfuls of Hickory or Cherry "CHIPS 'N CHUNKS" in the early stages of the drying cycle.

Wild, Wild Game Jerky

3.

Marinade/Brine in
¼ cup salt
¼ cup sugar
2 cups water
1 cup cider
1 cup soy sauce
1 oz. bourbon or brandy
½ tsp onion powder
½ tsp garlic powder
1 tsp M.S.G.
1 tsp grated fresh ginger
1 tsp grated orange peel
6 white cloves

Trim all fat from meat. Slice meat with the grain about ¼″ to ½″ thick. The meat slices nicely when semi-frozen or your butcher will slice it for you in his machine. Place meat in the cool marinade and leave overnight, or for no less than 8 hours.

Remove from brine and allow to air dry without rinsing. Smoke in your "LITTLE CHIEF" for 12 to 16 hours, depending on how dry you like the jerky. Use 3 panfuls of Hickory or Cherry "CHIPS 'N CHUNKS" in the early stages of the drying cycle.

24

Poker Party Jerky— Quick and Easy

4.

5 lbs chuck or shoulder roast about 1½" thick
½ cup non-iodized salt
½ cup sugar
1 qt. water

Slice beef into 1½" square chunks. Brine overnight in the refrigerator. Place on paper towels to dry for 1 hour. Do not rinse.

Smoke in your "Little Chief" for 8 hours, using 2 panfuls of Hickory flavor "Chips 'n Chunks." Remove from the smoker. Loosely wrap in aluminum foil and put in the refrigerator for 24 hours or more. Do not store for more than 7 days.

Slice thinly and serve with cheese, crackers and various sauces. Sensational!

Poker Party Jerky #2

5.

Marinade/Brine in
⅓ cup sugar
¼ cup salt
2 cups soy sauce
1 cup water
1 cup red wine
½ tsp onion powder
½ tsp pepper
½ tsp garlic powder
½ tsp tabasco sauce

Slice beef into 1½" square chunks. Brine overnight in the refrigerator. Place on paper towels to dry for 1 hour. Do not rinse.

Smoke in your "Little Chief" for 8 hours, using 2 panfuls of Hickory flavor "Chips 'n Chunks." Remove from the smoker. Loosely wrap in aluminum foil and put in the refrigerator for 24 hours or more. Do not store for more than 7 days.

Slice thinly and serve with cheese, crackers and various sauces. Sensational!

Snacky Sausage

(Dr. R. J. Hochhalter)

6.

5 lbs medium grade ground beef
5 rounded tsp Morton Tender Quick Salt
2-1/2 tsp Mustard Seed
3 tsp coarse ground pepper
1-1/2 tsp Garlic Powder
1-1/2 tsp Onion Powder

Mix all ingredients in large bowl, cover and refrigerate.

Next day, mix thoroughly again and refrigerate. Let set all of the next day (refrigerated). On the fourth day, form into 5 rolls. Place in Little Chief Smoker and smoke for 12 hours, using your choice of Little Chief "Chips 'n Chunks"—about 5 pans.

This sausage forms its own casings.

A note of warning—use only Tender Quick Salt and as specified; do not reduce the amount or proportion. However, the amounts of spices may be varied to suit your taste.

smoke flavoring of poultry and game birds

Smoking birds is fun. They are easy to prepare and their meat is rich and succulent to the taste. Smoked birds can be eaten hot from the oven or they will make marvelous hors d'oeuvres and snacks when eaten cold.

Smoked and cooked birds can be stored for several weeks in the refrigerator and are a good companion in a picnic basket or hiker's pack. A covered bowl of smoked and cooked chicken legs in the refrigerator will make you a hero with your family, and you'll find your culinary reputation soaring when you serve your guests smoked pheasant or squab with mild crackers and a dry white wine.

In this chapter, we'll get you started by reciting some basic smoke-flavoring suggestions for chicken and turkey. We can later refer back to these when we deal more specifically with the different types of wild bird.

Marinades and cooking procedures DO vary for domestic foul and wild birds, as the domestics seem to have a higher fat content and a generally milder taste.

DO USE the standard precautions of cleaning and handling when working with wild game. Pluck or skin and wash and cool as quickly as you can. We don't mean to be a bore, but to have a high quality finished product, we must have a high quality piece of meat to begin with.

You will see, because our recipes follow this pattern, it is a good practice to marinade the wild birds as the curing agents tend to tenderize the meat. The juices, herbs and spices color and tone the taste of the bird. Domestic birds and the smaller wild birds have a more delicate flavor and in most cases more subtle marinades or brines are used. Sometimes just a simple smoke-flavoring is the best.

■ Let's Get Started With a Few Smoke-Flavoring Recipes.

"Little Chief" Smoked Chicken and Chicken Parts

1. Simply section chicken as you desire, or leave whole, and place in your Little Chief with skin side down. Smoke for 45 minutes. Try Hickory "CHIPS 'N CHUNKS" the first time, but don't overlook Alder or Apple flavor.

When smoking is completed, prepare in your favorite way, reducing your cooking time by 20%.

"Little Chief" Hickory Flavored Turkey

2. When you can, get a 10 to 12 pound *fresh* turkey. If you use a frozen one, it must be fully thawed before putting it into the smoker. When smoking whole, open bird up as much as you can to allow smoke flavor to circulate freely over entire body and through cavities. Smoke with Hickory for 2 hours or until 2 panfuls are exhausted.

Remove the turkey from the smoker and cook in your favorite way. If you desire more smoke flavor, simply increase smoking time and amount of flavor fuel used. Your turkey will accept a great deal of flavor but be careful not to dry it too much.

Reduce your cooking time by 10% for each hour in the smoker. (Up to 40%.) Do not use more than 4 panfuls of "Chips 'n Chunks" flavor fuel.

"Easy Cure" Brine for Chicken and Small Wild Birds

(pheasant, quail, grouse, chicken, dove, partridge, squab, capon, etc.)

3.
½ cup non-iodized salt
½ cup white sugar
1 qt. water

Place birds in cool brine for 6 hours. Rinse and dry on paper towels for 1 hour. Smoke with 2 panfuls of Hickory flavor "Chips 'n Chunks" for 2 to 4 hours.

Remove from smoker and cook until done in the oven wrapped in foil.

Birds may now be eaten cold or warm and served with a light glaze, sauce or gravy. Use your imagination.

Sportsman's Brine for Chicken and Small Wild Birds

4.
¼ cup water
¼ cup soy sauce
¼ cup dry white wine
¼ cup brown sugar
½ tsp onion powder
½ tsp garlic powder
½ tsp ground ginger

Use this marinade recipe and proceed as in recipe #3 above. Try Apple "Chips 'n Chunks."

Apple Flavored Turkey or Cornish Game Hens

5.

Brine:
½ cup salt
½ cup sugar
1 qt. apple or cranberry juice
1 Tbsp rosemary
1 Tbsp sweet basil
Honey for basting

Place turkey in brine for 8 to 12 hours. Remove from brine. Rinse and air dry. Preheat your Little Chief smoker and place the turkey on the rack. (Open upper and lower cavities to expose insides to smoke flavor.) Smoke flavor with Apple "Chips 'n Chunks" for 30 minutes per pound or a maximum of 3 panfuls. (3 to 3½ hours.)

Remove from smoker and bake in the oven at 300° about 15 minutes per pound. Baste with honey the last hour of cooking.

Maple Flavored Turkey

6.

Brine:
½ cup salt
⅓ cup brown sugar
½ tsp maple flavoring
1 tsp onion powder
1 tsp celery salt
1 bay leaf, crushed
1 cup white dry wine
1 Tbsp pepper
3 cups water

Brine turkey and smoke flavor as in the above recipe, using Hickory or Cherry flavored "Chips 'n Chunks."

Bake as above, basting with maple pancake syrup once during last hour of cooking.

NOTE: Maple pancake syrup can replace brown sugar and maple flavoring in the brine.

Cherry Flavored Duck

7.

3 young ducks, halved or quartered
1 cup red wine
1 tsp fresh ginger
1 tsp dry mustard
⅓ cup brown sugar

Trim off fat and smoke flavor duck for 2 to 3 hours in the Little Chief smoker using Cherry wood for flavor.

Remove from the smoker and marinate in mixture of above ingredients overnight.

Barbeque until done (45 to 60 min). Baste with marinade while broiling.

28

Smoked Goose, Duck

8.

Brine:
¼ cup brown sugar
¼ cup salt
1 cup soy sauce
1 tsp onion powder
1 tsp garlic powder (optional)
½ cup sherry
2 Tbsp grated ginger root
½ cup orange juice
1½ cups water

Trim skin and fat. Puncture fatty areas with a fork or ice pick.

Brine overnight.

Rinse and dry on paper towels for 30 minutes. Place in the Little Chief for 2½ to 3 hours using 2 panfuls of Cherry, Apple or Hickory flavor "Chips 'n Chunks." Finish cooking in the oven at 300°.

Smoked Duck a' l'Orange (2 Ducks)

9.

flour
butter
1 cup white table wine
1 bay leaf
1 small onion
1 tsp salt
1 sprig parsley
3 peppercorns
2 oranges

Cut the smoked birds (refer to recipe #4 this chapter) in pieces and rub with flour. Cook in butter until lightly browned. Add wine, bay leaf, onion, salt, parsley and peppercorns. Cover and cook slowly until tender.

Remove duck to a warm platter. Strain sauce, adding the juice and the shredded zest (outer peel) of 2 oranges. Pour back on duck, heat and serve garnished with sliced peeled oranges.

Pecan-Stuffed Smoked Pheasant

10.

¼ cup butter
1⅓ cups dry bread crumbs
⅔ cup coarsely broken pecan meats
2 smoked pheasants (refer to recipe #4, this chapter)
2 Tbsp flour
¾ tsp salt
¼ tsp pepper
¼ cup butter
1½ cups hot water
⅓ cup sherry

Melt the 4 Tbsp butter and pour over bread crumbs. Add pecan meats and toss lightly. Stuff mixture into pheasants and truss birds. Combine the flour, salt and pepper, and lightly sprinkle over pheasants. Melt the other 4 Tbsp butter in a heavy frying pan. Brown each pheasant on all sides and transfer to a roasting pan. Add hot water and sherry to the browned birds. Cover and bake at 350° for 1 hour.

Baste with liquid every 15 minutes. Remove cover and continue baking for 20 minutes, or until the birds are crisp and brown. Remove birds to a platter and keep hot while you thicken drippings for gravy. Serves 6.

Smoked Chicken Breasts in Ham

11.

Remove skin and bones from 4 large chicken breasts. Cut meat in strips about 1 inch wide. Place on oiled screen in pre-heated Little Chief smoker for 1 pan full of Apple Chips 'n Chunks. Remove from smoker.

Dredge in a mixture of $\frac{1}{2}$ tsp each garlic salt and paprika, $\frac{1}{4}$ tsp chili powder and $\frac{1}{4}$ cup flour. Brown strips in 3 Tbsp butter. Add $\frac{2}{3}$ cup chicken broth or white table wine, cover, and simmer for 20 minutes or until tender. Cool. Wrap each piece of chicken in strips of thinly sliced baked ham. Skewer with cocktail picks. Wrap and carry in a cooler to the picnic.

NOTE: Arrange with avocado halves on one side and herb-buttered bread on the other. Take your prettiest tray along for this. Complete your picnic with fresh strawberries and champagne. Zowie!

"Little Chief" Jiffy Smoked Turkey or Chicken

12.

Place pre-cooked turkey or chicken in open greased baking dish that will fit in the Little Chief and smoke for 1 pan full of Apple flavor. Remove from smoker and serve. Use in salads, sandwiches, gravy, casseroles, etc.

"Little Chief" Smoked Chicken Salad

13.

$2\frac{1}{2}$ cups chicken (cooked)
1 small can pineapple tidbits, (drained)
1 cup diced celery
3 Tbsp lemon juice
$\frac{1}{4}$ tsp salt
slivered almonds
5 Tbsp mayonnaise

Cut cooked chicken into $\frac{1}{2}$" squares. Spread chicken on racks covered with a screen and smoke flavor with Apple or Cherry flavor "Chips 'n Chunks" for 45 minutes.

Mix chicken with next 4 ingredients and marinate for 1 hour. Add mayonnaise and mix well. Serve on lettuce leaves and sprinkle with $\frac{1}{4}$ cup almonds.

You can take your own favorite meat salads and by smoke-flavoring the meats, add new exciting flavors.

30

hors d'oeuvres and other special treats

The earlier chapters gave you recipes for smoked fish, shellfish, beef, jerky and fowl; all of which make outstanding hors d'oeuvres. The following pages will give you some special recipes that are simple to prepare and delicious to taste. Most important, their distinctive flavors are not available by any other commercial medium. You have the exciting smokey flavors of Hickory, Apple, Alder and Cherry at your command. You are limited only by your imagination and spirit of culinary adventure.

Here are a few recipes for openers. Try these and then let your imagination soar.

1.
"Easy Cure" Beef Chunkies

Prepare as for Meat Jerky, chapter 5 recipe 1, cutting into 1 to 1½" chunks. (Page 21)

2.
Fiesta Beef Chunkies

Prepare as for Meat Jerky, chapter 5 recipe 2, cutting into 1 to 1½" chunks. (Page 22)

"Little Chief" Smokey Meatballs

3.
1 cup dry bread crumbs
(smoked)
3 cups milk
½ cup finely chopped
onions
2 Tbsp butter
2# smoked ground beef
(see chapter 5, recipe 5)
2 eggs
2 tsp salt
pepper
butter for frying

Soak crumbs in milk. Saute the ½ cup chopped onions in butter until tender. Combine soaked crumbs, onion, beef, eggs, salt and pepper and beat with an electric mixer until blended smooth and rather shiny. Chill for 1 hour. Form into balls, wetting your hands in cold water as you go.

Fry balls in a small amount of melted butter. Shake the pan occasionally. This helps to keep the balls round.

"Little Chief" Smokey Meatballs Waikiki

4.

2 Tbsp cornstarch
1 can (13½ ounces) pine-
  apple tidbits, drained
  (reserve syrup)
½ cup brown sugar
⅓ cup vinegar
1 Tbsp soy sauce
⅓ cup chopped green
  pepper

Using recipe for "Little Chief" Smokey Meatballs, prepare with the following sauce:

Mix cornstarch and sugar. Stir in reserved pineapple syrup, vinegar and soy sauce until smooth. Pour into skillet. Cook over medium heat, stirring constantly, until mixture thickens and boils. Boil and stir 1 minute. Add meatballs, pineapple tidbits and green pepper. Heat through.

Smokey Meatballs Italiano

5.

1 onion minced
1 clove garlic, pressed
1 Tbsp olive oil
2 cans tomato paste
1½ qts water
  salt and pepper to taste
1 tsp chili powder
1 tsp sugar
1 Tbsp sweet basil
1 Tbsp oregano

In heavy pot, cook onion and garlic until soft in the olive oil. Add all ingredients and mix well. Simmer for ½ hour. Add meat balls and heat an additional ½ hour until sauce thickens. Serve as hors d'oeuvres with toothpicks or serve over pasta for spaghetti.

"Little Chief" Smokey Franks

6.

Purchase 1 package of good quality franks. Cut into bite size pieces and Hickory smoke for 35 minutes. Serve hot on cocktail picks with any of the sauces in the above 3 recipes.

"Little Chief" Vienna Sausage

7.

Prepare as for franks, using Apple or Alder smoke flavor.

**"Little Chief"
Spam 'n Bif
Chunkies**

8. Cube Spam or Bif and smoke on a wire screen for 2 hours, using Alder "Chips 'n Chunks." To serve, lightly saute in butter and serve warm.

**Sesame Pork
Chunkies**

9.
½ cup soy sauce
½ cup dry sherry
2 cloves garlic
1 Tbsp dry mustard
1 tsp ginger

Trim fat from smoked meat. Cut into chunks and marinate in combination of above ingredients. You should marinate the chunks for at least 6 hours.

Serve with hot mustard and sesame seeds.

**"Little Chief"
Smokey
Cocktail Shrimp
(Prawns)**

10. Spread fresh cooked or canned shrimp on oiled screen and smoke for 25 minutes with Hickory Flavor "Chips 'n Chunks." Serve chilled in cocktail sauce or heated in a favorite chili sauce of your own.

**Sesame
Smoked Shrimp**

11. Push cocktail picks through cooked, smoked shrimp or prawns. Dip in soy sauce and then into sesame seeds. The soy sauce will make the seeds adhere to the shrimp.

**Baha Shrimp
Kebobs**

12. Marinate smoked shrimp in tangy bottled chili sauce for 1 hour. Arrange on bamboo skewers with small pieces of green pepper and whole mushrooms. Dip sauce before barbequeing or broiling.

**Apple Smoked
Shrimp Scampi**

13.
⅛ tsp garlic, minced
2 Tbsp chopped fresh
parsley
½ cup white dry table wine
4 Tbsp butter
2 cups smoked shrimp
(medium large) smoked
30 or 35 minutes

Saute garlic and parsley in wine and butter. Heat to simmering; add smoked shrimp and simmer until heated through. Serve with rice as a main dish or in a chafing dish as hors d'oeuvres.

"Little Chief" Smoked Liver Pate

14.

1 lb. smoked chicken liver
(see recipe 16, chapter 4,
omit seasonings and do
not cook)
½ lb. sliced bacon
1 large onion
4 cloves garlic
4 bay leaves
1 tsp salt
¼ tsp red pepper
2 Tbsp Lea & Perrins
½ tsp nutmeg
1 tsp mustard
⅛ tsp ground cloves

Put liver in a covered pan with cut-up bacon. Add bay leaves, onion, garlic, salt, pepper and Lea & Perrins. Bring this to a boil and cook for twenty minutes in just enough water to cover. When done, discard bay leaves; add remaining ingredients and put in blender, then in molds. This will keep in the refrigerator for a week and it will also freeze well.

"Little Chief" Smoked Eggs

15.

Hard boiled and carefully peeled eggs may be smoked for about 1 hour or until they are a rich amber color. Smoke in the "cool box" technique as illustrated at the end of this chapter. Use for deviled eggs, sliced on salads, or sprinkle quartered eggs with paprika and serve as hors d'oeuvres. For a real adventure, use goose or turkey eggs, and serve them deviled. Aw, come on...try it!

"Little Chief" Smoked Sunflower and Pumpkin Seeds

16.

Soak overnight in saline solution. Smoke as above until seeds are dry.

"Little Chief" Smoked Nuts

17.

almonds
walnuts
peanuts
cashews
Brazil nuts
canned mixed nuts
roasted chestnuts
etc.

Spread nuts on fine screen or on aluminum foil pierced with many holes. Smoke for 1 pan full and not more than 1 hour with your favorite flavor "Chips 'n Chunks." Like cheese, with too much smoke, nuts will take on a burned, sooty flavor.

To apply salt *before* smoking, soak nuts for a few minutes in a light saline solution. Drain and then smoke. Salt by shaking salt in a plastic bag after smoking. For a saltier taste, apply fine salt by shaking smoked nuts and salt in a plastic bag *after* smoking.

Smokey Salmon on Celery Sticks

18.

1 cup smoked flaked
   salmon
1 package cream cheese
   (3 oz.)
2 Tbsp mayonnaise
   salt
6 stalks crisp celery

Mix smoked flaked salmon with next 3 ingredients. Pack grooves of celery with mixture and cut into ¾″ pieces.

Smokey Clam Dip

19.

8 oz. cream cheese
1 6½ oz can minced
   clams, smoked, drained
   dash Worcestershire
   sauce
   dash lemon
   salt and pepper
⅛ tsp garlic powder

Smoke clams 15 or 20 minutes on an oiled screen using Apple or Alder "Chips 'n Chunks."

Mix clams with other ingredients and chill.

Smoked Popcorn/Wild Rice

20.

Smoke flavor 1 cup popcorn or wild rice for 30 minutes. Use mixture ⅔ Apple—⅓ Cherry "Chips 'n Chunks." Place in mason jar and add 2 tablespoons water, cranberry, pineapple, orange or other fruit juices (experiment to your taste) for each cup smoked corn or rice. Seal for 1 week. This replaces the moisture removed by "Little Chief" smoker and is required for good kernel popping. Pop in normal manner. Salt and butter to taste. You can't buy this in stores. Dynamite!

"Little Chief" Smokey Cheese

21.

Use any of the following harder cheeses: cheddar, jack, Swiss, beer, etc. Section into cubes approximately 1½″ thick. Place on wire grills or plastic hardware cloth and smoke in the "cool box" technique as illustrated below for 1 pan full of Hickory Flavor (about 50 minutes). Cover and allow cubes to set for an hour at room temperature before serving.

Cut cubes into halves or quarters at a fancy angle for nifty color shadings. Use smoked cheese in your favorite spreads or cheese ball.

Softer cheeses may be left in larger sections and wrapped in cheese cloth before smoking. Smoke with Apple "Chips 'n Chunks" for 30 minutes only.

Strong cheeses such as Roquefort, limburger, blue, etc. may not lend themselves to smoking as well, but if you're a real cheese nut, try it.

"Cool Box" Smoking Technique

22.

Instructions for "cool box" technique for smoking with less heat.

1. Remove smoker from box and rack from smoker.
2. Place two 16″ sticks, 1″ square (or close) across the top of the smoker body.
3. Place rack with product to be smoked on top of the sticks.
4. Place smoker box, UPSIDE-DOWN, over the rack and allow to rest on the sticks, also.
5. Smoke as per recipe instructions.

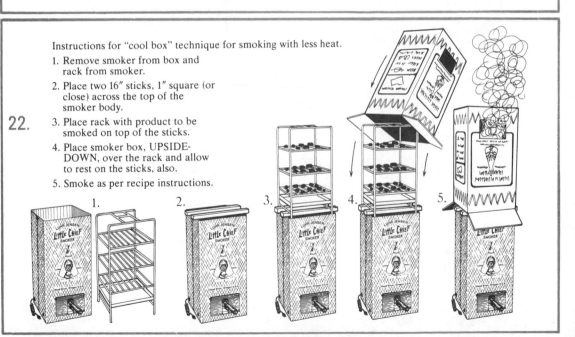

36

smoke flavored noodles, macaroni, spaghetti, grains and breads

The addition of old-fashioned smoke flavors to your favorite casseroles, soups, salads or pasta dishes is easy with your Little Chief smoker and "Chips 'n Chunks" flavor fuels.

Simply follow the directions for flavoring the items listed below, and then use them in their usual way in your favorite dish. You'll be pleasantly surprised.

| Noodles | Macaroni | Spaghetti | Beans | Peas |
| Lentils | Rice | Wheat | Barley | Corn |

Cover the grills of your Little Chief smoker with a fine screen so that the small articles won't slip through the slots. Evenly spread the product on the screen, one layer deep for maximum smoke coverage. Smoke flavor with Hickory "Chips 'n Chunks" for 30 minutes. Try the other flavors. They are all good. Store your smoked product in air tight containers, and use freely in your favorite recipes.

*Some Suggested Uses:

Smokey pea soup	Hickory smoked lasagna	Smoked baked beans
Smokey bean soup	Hickory smoked spaghetti	Smokey marinated bean salad
Smokey lentil soup	Smoked macaroni salad	Smoked wild wheat
Smokey corn chowder	Smoked macaroni & cheese	Smoked wild barley
Smokey bean patties	Hickory smoked fried rice	Smoked Pilaf

■ **Here are a Few Recipes that We Especially Like**

Smokey Bean Patties
(Vegetarian's Delight)

1.

1 cup dry smoked beans (navy, lima or pinto)
3 cups water
1 chopped onion
¼ cup chopped parsley
2 egg yolks
2 Tbsp cream or canned milk
¼ tsp pepper
1 tsp salt

Bring beans to a boil in the water. Lower heat and simmer until tender. Drain off liquid. Grind or mash beans and add onion and parsley.

Beat and add remaining ingredients. Shape into balls and flatten into patties. Chill. Dip patties in flour and smoked bread crumbs. Saute slowly in butter. Serve with catsup or barbeque sauce.

37

Smokey Chili Con Carne

2.

2 cups dry smoked
   kidney or pinto beans
½ cup chopped onion
3 Tbsp fat
1½ lbs. smoked hamburger
   (see meat section for
   instructions)
1¼ cups canned tomatoes
1 tsp or more salt
½ bay leaf
1 tsp sugar
1 to 2 Tbsp chili powder

Cook smoked beans until tender following package directions. Drain off and save excess water until water level is just covering beans.

Saute onion in fat. Add smoked hamburger. Stir and saute until meat is well done. Add beans and remaining ingredients. Cover and cook slowly for 1 hour, adding bean liquid as needed.

Serve with tortilla chips or saltines.

Smokey Lentil Soup

3.

2 cups smoked lentils
2 qts. water
2 slices raw bacon, diced
1 medium onion, sliced
¼ cup chopped carrots
½ cup chopped celery
3 Tbsp chopped parsley
1 clove minced garlic
1 tsp salt
¼ tsp black pepper
½ tsp oregano
1 can tomatoes (#1)
1 Tbsp wine vinegar

Simmer first 11 ingredients for 1½ hours. Add tomatoes and break them up with a spoon. Add wine vinegar and simmer 30 minutes.

Smokey Meat Loaf

4.

In your favorite meat loaf recipe, try ½ cup half-cooked smoked rice per pound of meat. This gives a delicious flavor and retains juices in the loaf.

* NOTE: Half-cooked rice is prepared in ½ the usual amount of water in ½ the normal cooking time. It will finish cooking in your main dish and will absorb many nutritious juices that are usually lost as excess liquid. Use also in stuffings.

38

Smokey Marinated Bean Salad

5.

1½ cups dry smoked beans
1 large chopped onion
1 cup salad oil
¼ cup red wine vinegar
1 tsp salt
½ tsp dry mustard
½ tsp pepper
½ tsp sugar
  garlic

Boil beans and let cool in liquid overnight. Add onions. Mix next 6 ingredients and pour over beans. Stir well and add 4 cloves garlic, each speared with a toothpick. Bury garlic in the salad. Cover and marinate in refrigerator a day or two before serving. (Remove garlic.)

Smoke Flavored Bread and Cracker Crumbs

6.

Smoked crumbs make excellent meat coatings for fried chicken, chicken fried steak, fried shrimp, etc.

Using a fine screen on the grills of your Little Chief smoker, spread the stale bread or crackers evenly and in one layer only. Smoke for 10 minutes only using Alder, Apple or Hickory flavored "Chips 'n Chunks." DO NOT OVERSMOKE, as the bread absorbs smoke quickly and tends to become bitter when too much smoke is applied.

When smoked to your taste, simply crush with a rolling pin.

Campbell's Chunky Soup with Smokey Macaroni

7.

1 can Campbell's
  Chunky Beef Soup
1 cup smoked macaroni
  elbows
½ can water
1 Tbsp red wine

Combine all ingredients and warm to a low simmer. A spicy, zesty taste treat!

IMPORTANT SAFEGUARDS

When operating your Little Chief™Smokehouse, please observe the following basic safety precautions:

- **Read all operating instructions thoroughly before using the smokehouse.**
- Your Little Chief™is designed **strictly for outdoor use.** Place it on a well-ventilated patio or car port with a non-combustible floor, out of the wind.
- Maintain a minimum of two feet clearance between the smokehouse and any adjacent material.
- **Improper use** (e.g. for purposes other than smoking fish, game or fowl, using liquids which would result in electrical shock, etc.) or use of accessories not recommended by the manufacturer (e.g. using the shipping carton as a heat shield around the smokehouse, which could potentially cause a fire) may cause hazards and void any warranties.
- **Maintain close supervision when the smokehouse is used near children or pets.**
- **Do not touch the smokehouse surfaces when it is in use.** It can be **hot** and could cause burns. Use a handle or knob.
- **Prevent electrical hazards.** Plug only into an approved, grounded outlet. Never immerse the cord, plug or heating element in water or other liquids. Keep it out of the rain, and don't expose it to moisture.
- Don't allow the cord to contact the edge of a counter, table or any hot surface.
- **Never operate your Little Chief™with a damaged electrical cord or outlet.** Have these or any other electrical problem checked by a competent electrician.
- If an extension cord must be used, make sure it is a UL approved, 3-prong (grounded) cord.
- **Unplug your smokehouse when it's not in use.**
- **Don't move your smokehouse while it is in use unless you have emptied the drip pan.** Don't place it on or near a hot gas or electric burner.
- Start each smoking session with a clean, empty drip pan. Spraying a non-stick coating such as Pam on the pan will facilitate cleanup. Check the drip pan every two or three hours (more often if smoking foods with a high fat content) to ensure it doesn't overflow onto the heating coil, possibly causing a fire.
- Unplug the smokehouse and allow it to cool before cleaning or performing any maintenance on components.
- Never leave your smokehouse unattended when it is in operation.

IMPORTANT: SAVE THESE INSTUCTIONS

OPERATING INSTRUCTIONS

Home Smoking: It's easy, it's inexpensive, and so-o delicious!

Your own, "old-fashioned country style" smoked fish...bacon or ham...jerky...pheasant or duck, is easily and economically achieved with the "Little Chief" electric smoker. Delicious smoke-house flavors of HICKORY, APPLE, CHERRY, and ALDER permeate the meats to add "mouth-watering" tastes that are not available with grocery store or expensive delicatessen products. The pleasures of the age-old art of curing and smoke-flavoring can be yours to enjoy at home with the simple and economical "Little Chief" electric smoker.

Curing and smoking of game and domestic meats is an ancient art, originally conceived as a means of food preservation. Curing meats with natural salt was used by the ancient Chinese and many western civilizations as early as 1,000 B.C. The introduction of salt to meats, while curing, causes the meat to undergo chemical changes resulting in greatly increased preservation.

When heat is introduced by means of low-temperature "oven" (smokehouses), the moisture is removed, the meat becomes firm and may then be easily stored for extended periods of time. The aroma of the woods used in heat generation permeates the meat with its own delicate flavor. This process imparts the subtle, yet tangy taste of hickory or other hardwood flavors that many of us have tasted in years gone by. Herbs and spices such as garlic, pepper, bay and dill may be introduced to your product by the dry cure or brining techniques which are explained in the recipe section of this booklet. Natural sweeteners such as maple, wild-honey, molasses, pineapple and brown sugar may also be used to flavor your gourmet treats.

Your "Little Chief" electric smoker, and recipes in this and other available booklets will provide you with a great deal of enjoyment as you turn out smoked delicacies that will delight you, your family and your friends.

Some tips on getting the most from your Little Chief Smoker.

Your smoker is a versatile cooking tool. Don't be afraid to use it...to experiment with it in many ways. The delicate smoke flavors of the four Chips n' Chunks™ fuels will add zest and tantalizing aromas to many of your favorite dishes. Renowned gourmet, James Beard, acclaims the "Little Chief" as being an indispensable part of his kitchen. Try his recipe for "Smoked Pork Loin," it would make anyone an instant believer.

The "Easy-Brine" solution mentioned earlier in the booklet can be modified to taste. The salt is the curing agent and the sugar adds flavor and color to the product. The introduction of herbs and spices is easy and exciting. Pepper on jerky is a natural. Garlic or onion powder on fish or morning sausage is a delectable taste treat. Imagine a turkey brine made of applejuice and rosemary, or a pork chop sweetened with honey or pineapple juice!

Keep your brine solutions in glass or crockery containers. Plastic and stainless is O.K. DO NOT USE ALUMINUM. A brine solution may be used several times when smoking large quantities, but keep your brine solutions cool and preferably in the refrigerator.

Spray your smoker grills and drip pan with "Pam" or other brand of non-stick coating. It helps, when cleaning.

Pick a good outside or well vented area for the actual smoking. The smoke is strong, and, by the way, your neighbors will be over to see "what's cookin'."!

Keep your smoker out of a direct breeze, heat in the smoking chamber can be lost if the smoker is not protected from the wind.

CHAPTER NINE
OPERATING INSTRUCTIONS
Ready? Here's how.

- **Remove Smoker from carton. Discard packing. Assemble Grills and Drip Pan per instructions.**
- **Choose an outside well-ventilated area, protected from wind and moisture.**

1. FILLET:
Section fish as shown and split at back bone. Remove all small bones and cut meat into easy-to-handle chunks. Remove all blood, ragged edges and wash thoroughly.

3. WASH & DRY:
Remove chunks from brine an⸍ rinse thoroughly in cool water. Place chunks on paper towels pat dry. Allow to air dry for a⸍ an hour. When you notice a ta⸍ glaze on the surface of the fis⸍ ready for loading.

2. BRINE
"Easy-Cure" brine solution consists of ½ cup non-iodized salt and ½ cup sugar, dissolved into one quart of water, with seasonings as desired. Immerse fish in glass, stainless or crockery container (not aluminum). Brine thin chunks 4 to 6 hours; thick chunks 8 to 12 hours, overnight is good, refrigerate if possible. Cool is the key.

4. RACK & LOAD
Place chunks on grills at prep⸍ tion area, then take rack and ⸍ (or grills alone, depending on⸍ Smoker model) to smoking s⸍ Slip rack or grills into smoke⸍ through top or through front⸍ (again depending on Smoker ⸍ and close lid or door. Smoker⸍ be preheated, or plugged in r⸍

5 FILL FLAVOR PAN:
Fill flavor pan with desired fuel and place onto heating element. One pan of fuel will start to burn in about 5 minutes and smoke briskly for about 45 minutes. Smoke flavoring is NOT needed throughout the entire drying cycle. Two or three panfuls are sufficient in most cases, even though total drying time may take up to 20 hours.

6. ENJOY
Thin fillets will be done in about 4 hours. Thick ones in about 8 to 10 hours. Check occasionally when nearing this time, Your fish should be nicely colored, flakey to the touch and de-licious!...allow to cool a bit and watch them disappear.

Suggestions on care, cleaning and storage.

Your "Little Chief" Electric Smoker has been quality designed to give you years of trouble-free enjoyment. With normal care, the lightweight body, rack and grills will last forever.

The grills and drip pan should be regularly cleaned. Simply brush the residue from them and slip them into the dishwasher. If possible, a light coating of "Pam" or other non-stick coating is good.

The rack and inside smoking chamber do not need cleaning, but, at your preference, an occasional wipe-down of the smoke residue certainly will not hurt.

Store your "Little Chief" in a dry area. And be sure to replace the flavor pan, or the grills and drip pan which you've just put into the dishwasher.

Your "Little Chief" Electric Smoker will give you many years of pleasure. Use it and enjoy!

send us your favorite smoker recipes

We at Luhr Jensen and Sons, Inc. are constantly learning new uses for the "Little Chief" smoker. When we first started, we primarily used the smoker for curing and smoking with old time recipes. Soon, we learned that the smoke-flavoring of fresh meats, before the conventional cooking methods, added the exciting fresh smoked flavors to all of our favorite meat recipes. We also found that by smoke-flavoring noodles, macaroni, grains and bread that we could add the fresh-smoked flavors of Hickory, Apple, Cherry and Alder to many other dishes such as soups, casseroles, stuffings, and many hors d'oeuvres delicacies.

Using the many techniques outlined in this book, we feel that new recipes and alternate methods of using the "Little Chief" smoker are sure to be discovered. If *you* have a recipe or a suggestion as to how others might enjoy their smoker more, we would like to hear from you. At a future time, we will compile these submissions and publish a second "Little Chief" recipe book that will offer a wide range of proven recipes for the wonderful art of smoke-cooking.

Please send your recipes on an 8½ x 11 typewritten page, together with the release statement as recited below. If we use your recipe or suggestion, we will credit you in the book and send you a free copy upon publication.

THANKS!

Sincerely,

Luhr Jensen

Luhr Jensen and Sons, Inc.

RELEASE STATEMENT
I authorize use of my name for credit and the publication of my recipe in any Luhr Jensen and Sons, Inc. publication. I understand that I will receive a free copy of any such publication for my personal use. This recipe becomes the property of Luhr Jensen and Sons, Inc. and will not be returned.

Another quality product from the folks at Luhr Jensen.

Thanks for buying this quality Luhr Jensen product. We are especially proud of our "Little Chief" smoker. As you will experience, it's a special product, designed to give pleasure to the whole family. The thrill of the catch can be relived and shared while the fisherman or hunter, with his family and friends, enjoys the bounty he has provided. Smoked fish, jerky, or the many taste treats that your "Little Chief" enables you to create, will provide you with satisfaction and pleasure for many years to come.

Luhr Jensen

Warranty
(Limited)

Luhr Jensen products are expertly assembled with the finest materials available. We take great pride in our "LITTLE CHIEF" smoker and wish to insure your continued pleasure with our products.

Within one year from the purchase date of your "LITTLE CHIEF" smoker Luhr Jensen & Sons will, to the original owner, repair or replace any part that proves to be defective due to faulty material or workmanship.

The "LITTLE CHIEF" smoker is designed with separate easily replaceable parts. Should they require service remove the defective part and return prepaid to:

Luhr Jensen & Sons, Inc.
Claim Dept. POBX 297
Hood River, Oregon 97031

All claims submitted must be accompanied with an explanation of defect, date and place of purchase. This warranty void in cases of abuse, misuse, accident or commercial application. Liability limited to original purchase price.

For smokers not within warranty coverage, parts may be ordered at a nominal charge.

SEND $1.00 to LUHR JENSEN, DEPT. LCRB for a complete, illustrated catalog of all products.

Replacement Parts and Wood Flavor Fuels

Your Owner's Literature packet contains a separate Replacement Parts Order Form, and a list of the complete line of Little Chief Smoker products. Where not available from a local source, all of these can be purchased directly from us.

The prices listed are necessarily applicable for a twelve month period following the stated effective date. After this time, orders will be filled and shipped to you C.O.D. at the current prices.

Other Little Chief Smoker models and Wood Flavor Fuels are illustrated and described on the following pages.

When ordering, include the Stock Number of the product.

For more information write: Little Chief Smoker Products,
                                   c/o Luhr Jensen & Sons, Inc.
                                   P.O. Box 297
                                   Hood River, Oregon 97031